11+

NON-VERBAL REASONING

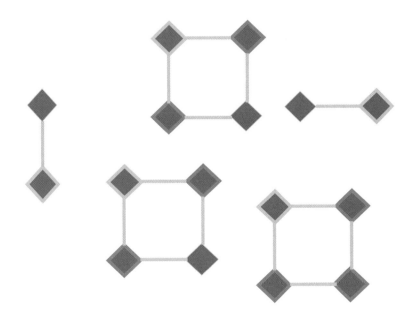

Practice and Tests for the
GL Assessment
11+ Test

Ages 10–11

Practice

SCHOLASTIC

Published in the UK by Scholastic, 2023

Scholastic Distribution Centre, Bosworth Avenue, Tournament Fields, Warwick, CV34 6UQ

Scholastic Ireland, 89E Lagan Road, Dublin Industrial Estate, Glasnevin, Dublin, D11 HP5F

SCHOLASTIC and associated logos are trademarks and/or registered trademarks of Scholastic Inc.

© Scholastic, 2023

A CIP catalogue record for this book is available from the British Library.

ISBN 978-0702-31955-6

Printed by Ashford Colour Press

The book is made of materials from well-managed, FSC®-certified forests and other controlled sources.

1 2 3 4 5 6 7 8 9   3 4 5 6 7 8 9 0 1 2

Authors

Nicola Palin with thanks to Jon Palin

Editorial team

Rachel Morgan, Vicki Yates, Kate Baxter, Julia Roberts and Jennie Clifford

Design team

Andrea Lewis and Couper Street Type Co.

Illustration

Couper Street Type Co.

Contents

 Extended answers can be found online
www.scholastic.co.uk/pass-your-11-plus/extras/gl

About the GL Assessment Test

About the GL Assessment Test

The Granada Learning (GL) Assessment is one of the leading providers of the tests that grammar schools use in selecting students at 11+. The GL Assessment test assesses students' ability in verbal reasoning, non-verbal reasoning, mathematics and English. Children typically take the GL Assessment test at the start of Year 6.

Students answer multiple-choice questions and record their answers on a separate answer sheet. This answer sheet is then marked via OMR (Optical Mark Recognition) scanning technology.

The structure and contents of the test can vary. Sometimes a separate paper is done per subject and sometimes papers are combined.

The English part of the test includes comprehension and spelling, punctuation and grammar questions. Verbal reasoning tends to include questions looking at word meanings, making words, relationships between numbers, and codes.

The mathematics tests are in line with the National Curriculum up to the start of Year 6. Questions will use knowledge of times tables, mental arithmetic, using the four operations, reading graphs, and shape, space and measure. Non-verbal reasoning focuses on processing graphic information, following patterns, applying maths skills (rotation, reflection, symmetry) and applying logical thinking and problem-solving skills.

The other main provider of 11+ tests is CEM. The CEM test assesses the same subjects as GL and uses a multiple-choice format.

How to Use the Book

Scholastic 11+ Non-verbal Reasoning Practice and Test for the GL Assessment Ages 10–11 is part of the *Pass Your 11+* series. The practice questions in this book have been designed to accurately reflect the format and style of the GL Assessment test.

The book offers:

- A practice section with questions categorised by topic area.

- Three practice papers with timings for each paper.

- Multiple-choice questions to practise answering the types of question your child will meet in their GL Assessment test.

- Extended answers with explanations provided at www.scholastic.co.uk/pass-your-11-plus/extras/gl or via the QR code opposite.

You can work through the book in order or choose topics based on areas your child needs more support with. You can take a practice paper at any time to help decide which areas need practice.

Progress Tracker

Record your marks to track your progress.

		Marks
Practice	Series	/16
	Analogies	/13
	Like Figures (Two)	/8
	Like Figures (Three)	/8
	Codes (In a Box)	/8
	Codes (Two and Three Letter)	/8
	Odd One Out	/13
	Matrices	/13
	Merge Shapes (Hidden)	/4
	Merge Shapes (Addition)	/4
	Merge Shapes (Subtraction)	/4
	Cubes (Which Net?)	/8
	Cubes (Which Cube?)	/8
	Folding and Punching	/6
	Reflections	/3
	Rotations	/4
	3D Shapes	/8
Practice Papers	Paper 1	/26
	Paper 2	/23
	Paper 3	/23

Series

There are five squares arranged in order with one square left empty. One of the five squares on the right replaces the empty square on the left to complete the sequence.
Circle the correct answer.

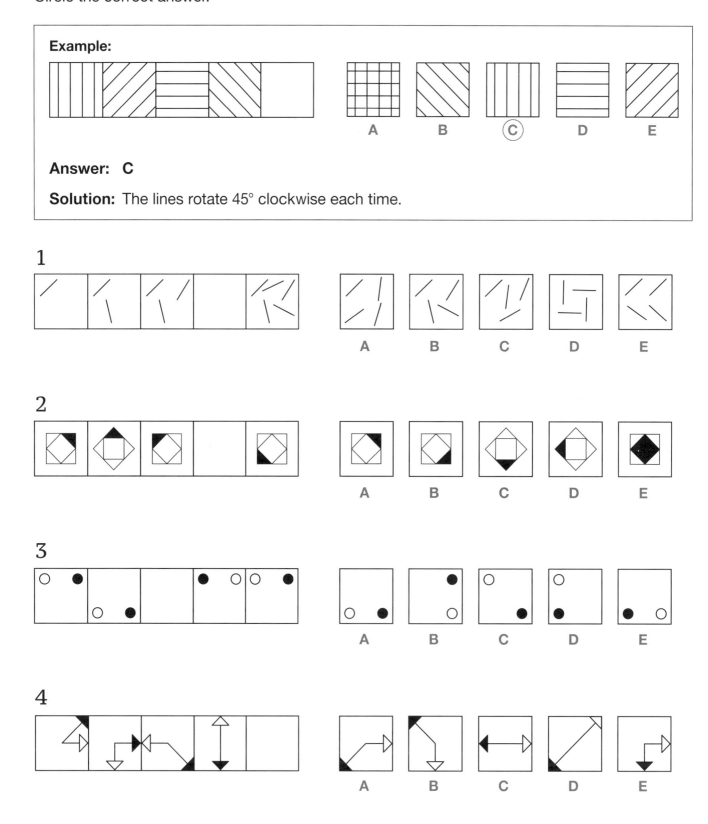

Example:

Answer: C

Solution: The lines rotate 45° clockwise each time.

1

2

3

4

5

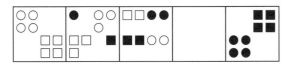

A　　B　　C　　D　　E

6

A　　B　　C　　D　　E

7

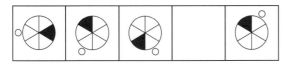

A　　B　　C　　D　　E

8

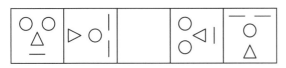

A　　B　　C　　D　　E

9

A　　B　　C　　D　　E

10

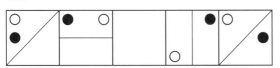

A　　B　　C　　D　　E

11

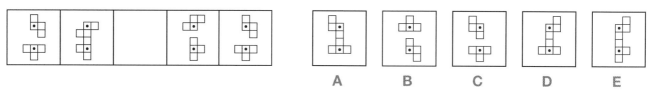

12

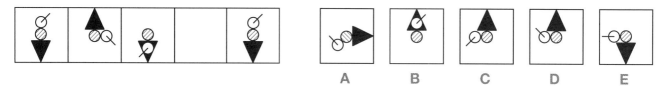

13

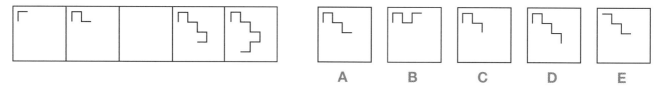

14

15

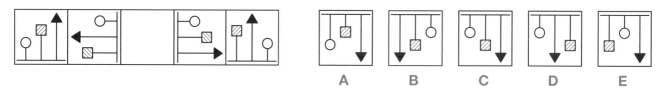

16

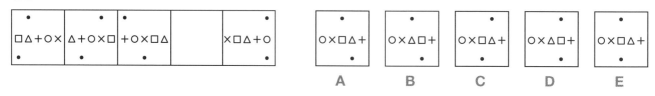

Analogies

On the left there are two shapes with an arrow between them. Decide what changes have been made to the shape on the left to create the shape on the right. Then look at the third shape, the arrow next to it and five more shapes. Decide which of the five shapes completes the second pair in the same way as the first pair. Circle the correct answer.

Example:

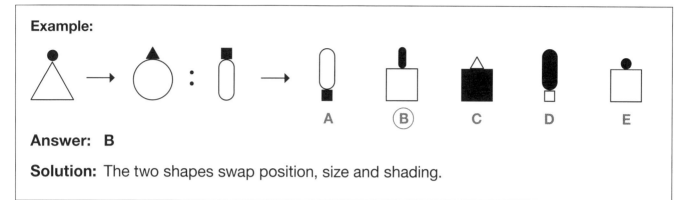

Answer: B

Solution: The two shapes swap position, size and shading.

1

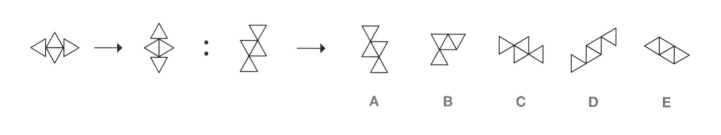

2

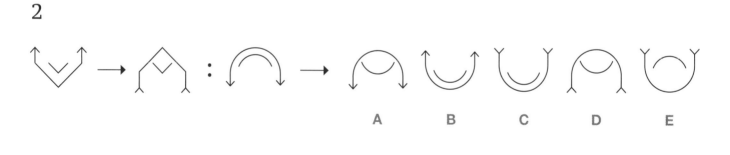

3

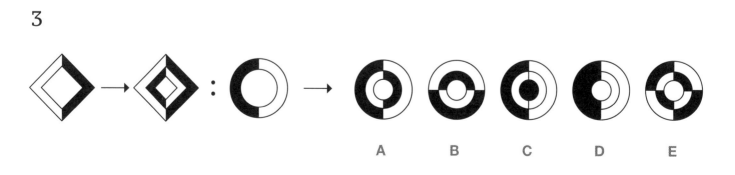

4

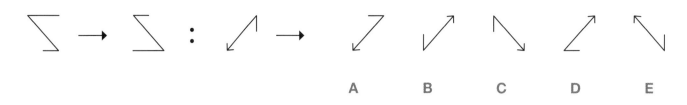

A   B   C   D   E

5

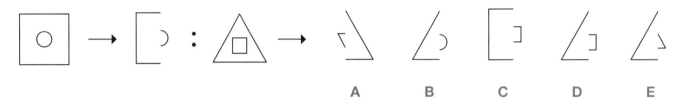

A   B   C   D   E

6

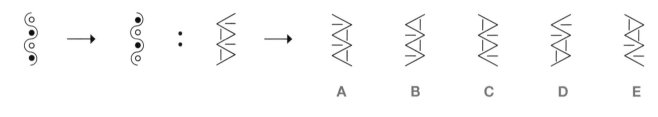

A   B   C   D   E

7

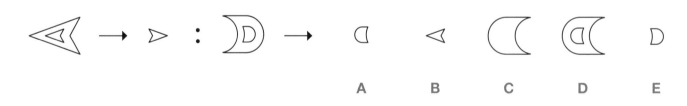

A   B   C   D   E

8

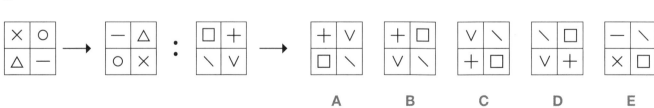

A   B   C   D   E

9

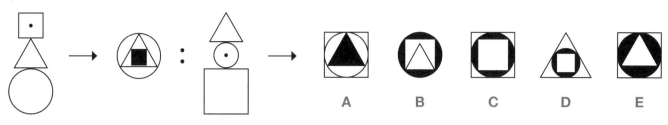

10

11

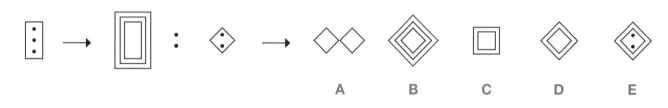

12

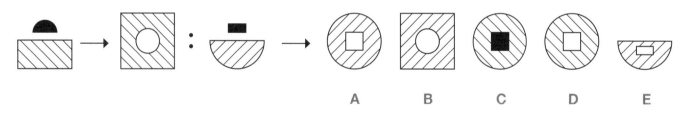

13

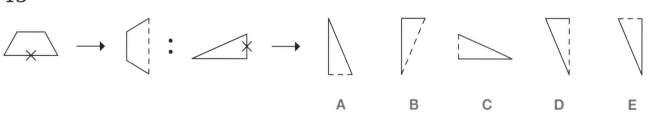

Like Figures (Two)

On the left there are two figures that are alike. On the right, one of the five figures is most like the two figures on the left. Circle the correct answer.

Example:

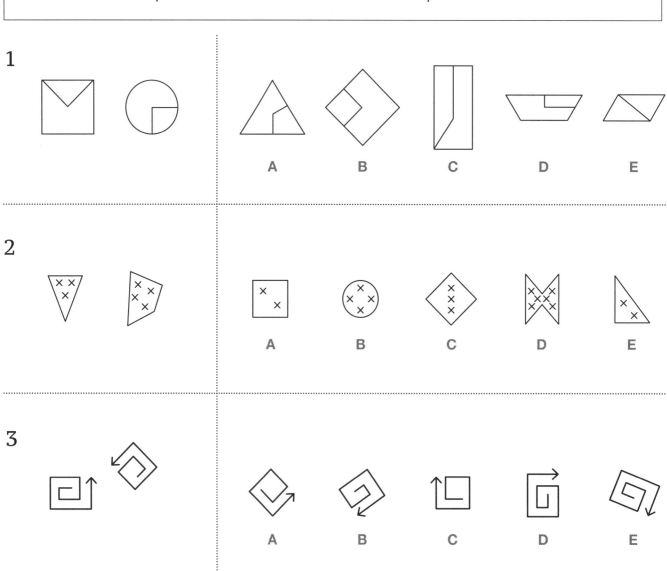

Answer: E

Solution: Each shape has two lines and a dot near the midpoint of the two ends.

4

A   B   C   D   E

5

A   B   C   D   E

6

    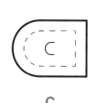

A   B   C   D   E

7

    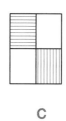 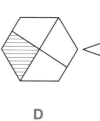 

A   B   C   D   E

8

A   B   C   D   E

Like Figures (Three)

On the left there are three figures that are alike. On the right, one of the five figures is most like the three figures on the left. Circle the correct answer.

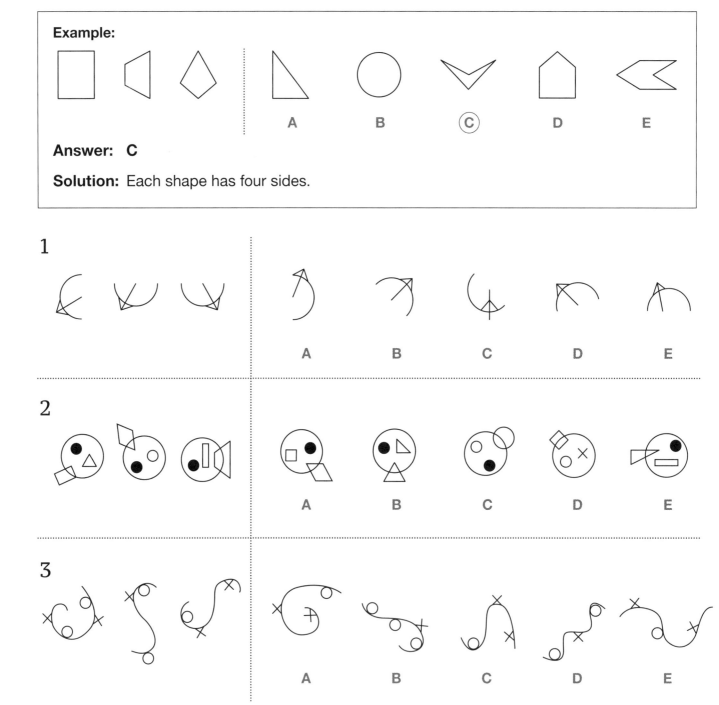

Example:

A   B   C   D   E

Answer: C

Solution: Each shape has four sides.

1

A   B   C   D   E

2

A   B   C   D   E

3

A   B   C   D   E

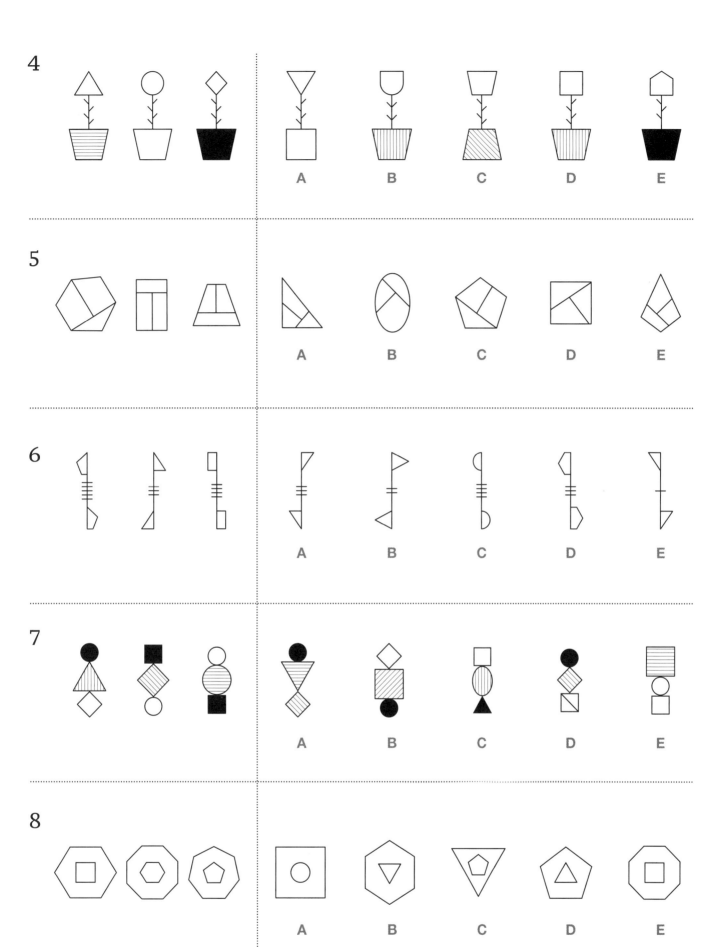

Codes (In a Box)

On the left are some shapes and their codes. You must find out what each code letter represents. Then find the correct code for the last shape from the set of five codes on the right. Circle the correct answer.

Example:

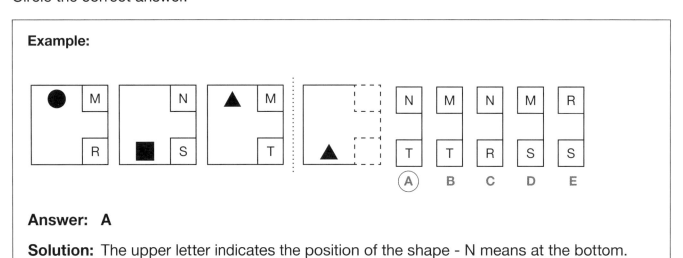

Answer: A

Solution: The upper letter indicates the position of the shape - N means at the bottom. The lower letter indicates the type of shape - T means a triangle.

1

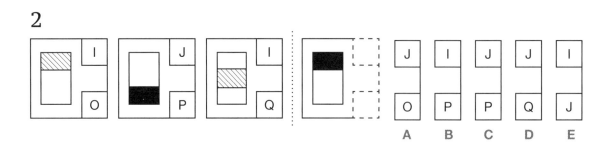

2

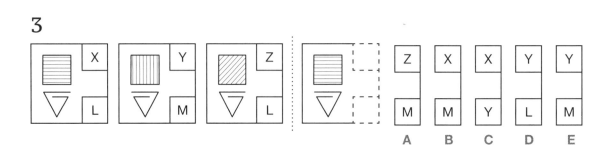

3

4

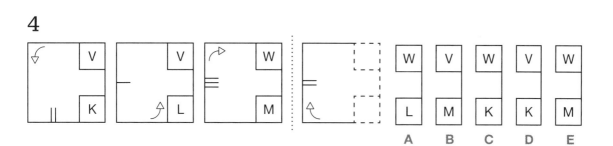

5

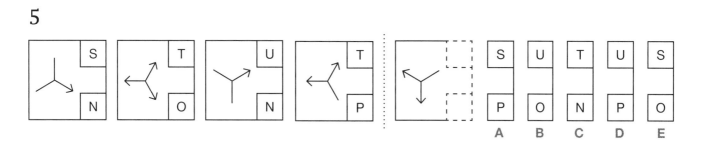

6

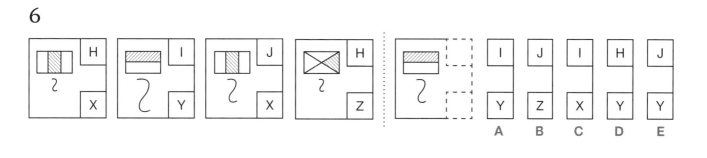

7

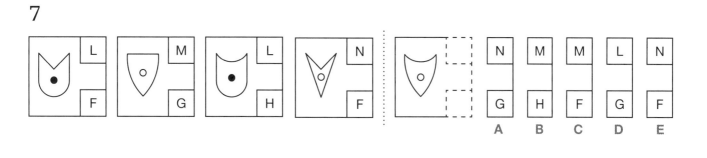

8

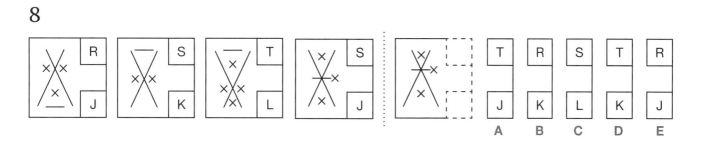

Codes (Two and Three Letters)

On the left are some shapes and their codes. You must find out what each code letter represents. Then find the correct code for the last shape from the set of five codes on the right. Circle the correct answer.

Example:

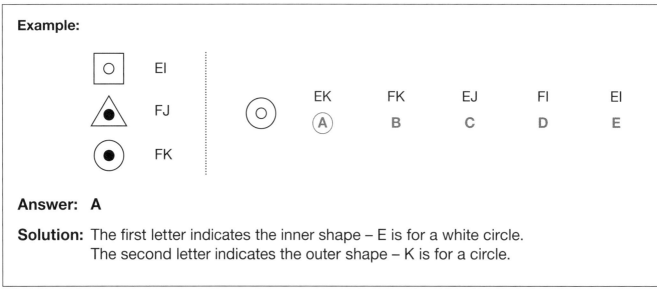

EK   FK   EJ   FI   EI

A   B   C   D   E

Answer: A

Solution: The first letter indicates the inner shape – E is for a white circle.
The second letter indicates the outer shape – K is for a circle.

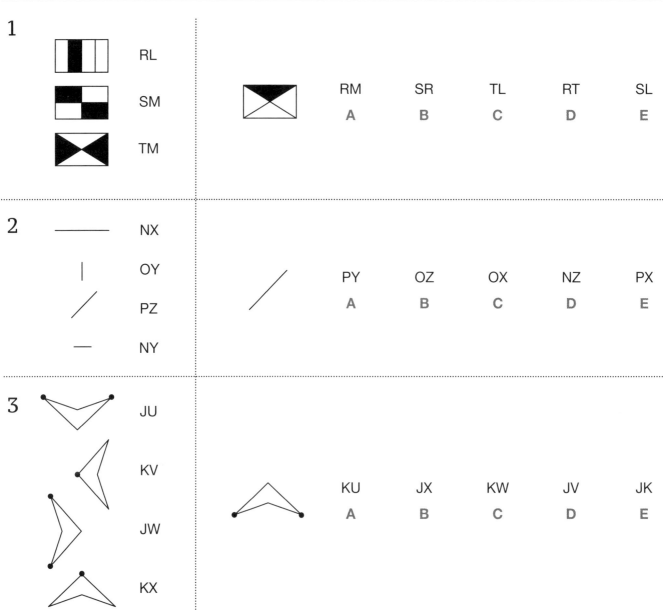

1

RM   SR   TL   RT   SL

A   B   C   D   E

2

PY   OZ   OX   NZ   PX

A   B   C   D   E

3

KU   JX   KW   JV   JK

A   B   C   D   E

4

NX

NY

OZ

	OX	NO	ON	OY	NZ
	A	**B**	**C**	**D**	**E**

5

KFR

LGS

MFS

	LFR	MGR	KGS	LFS	KFS
	A	**B**	**C**	**D**	**E**

6

JGY

KHZ

KIY

	KGZ	JHY	JGZ	KHY	JIY
	A	**B**	**C**	**D**	**E**

7

PSV

QTW

RTX

PUW

	RUV	QSX	PTV	QUX	RSW
	A	**B**	**C**	**D**	**E**

8

FRT

GSU

FSV

HRV

	GRU	FST	HST	GRT	FRV
	A	**B**	**C**	**D**	**E**

Odd One Out

There are five figures and one of them is most unlike the other four, making it the odd one out. Circle the correct answer.

Example:

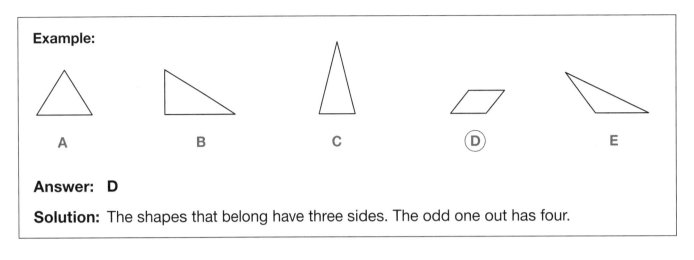

A   B   C   (D)   E

Answer: D

Solution: The shapes that belong have three sides. The odd one out has four.

1

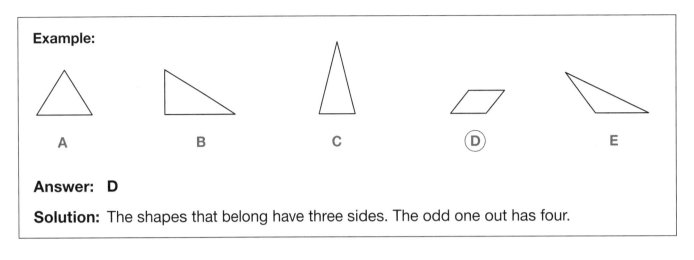

A   B   C   D   E

2

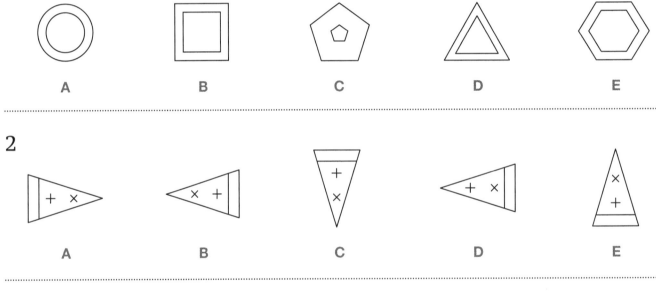

A   B   C   D   E

3

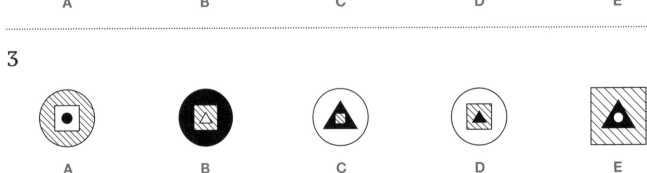

A   B   C   D   E

4

    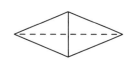

A   B   C   D   E

5

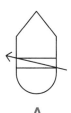  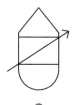   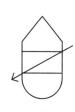

A   B   C   D   E

6

A   B   C   D   E

7

A   B   C   D   E

8

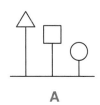

A   B   C   D   E

9

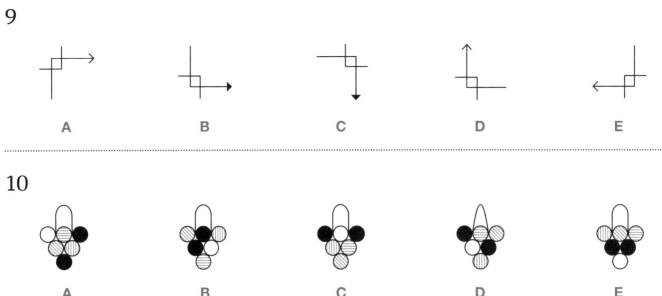

A   B   C   D   E

10

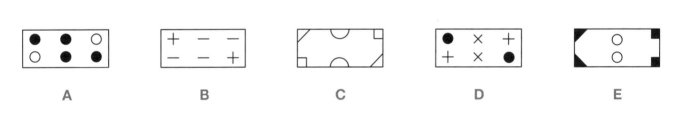

A   B   C   D   E

11

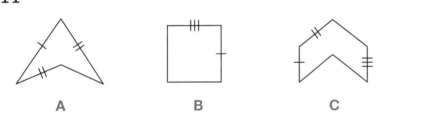

A   B   C   D   E

12

A   B   C   D   E

13

A   B   C   D   E

Matrices

The big square on the left contains either four or nine small squares, including one that is empty. One of the five small squares on the right will fill the empty square.
Circle the correct answer.

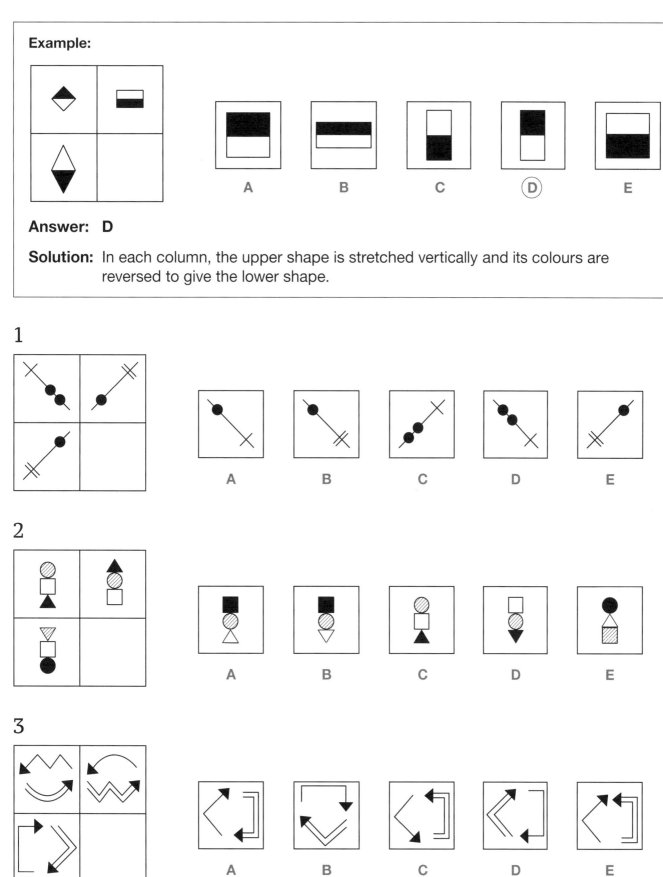

Example:

Answer: D

Solution: In each column, the upper shape is stretched vertically and its colours are reversed to give the lower shape.

1

2

3

4

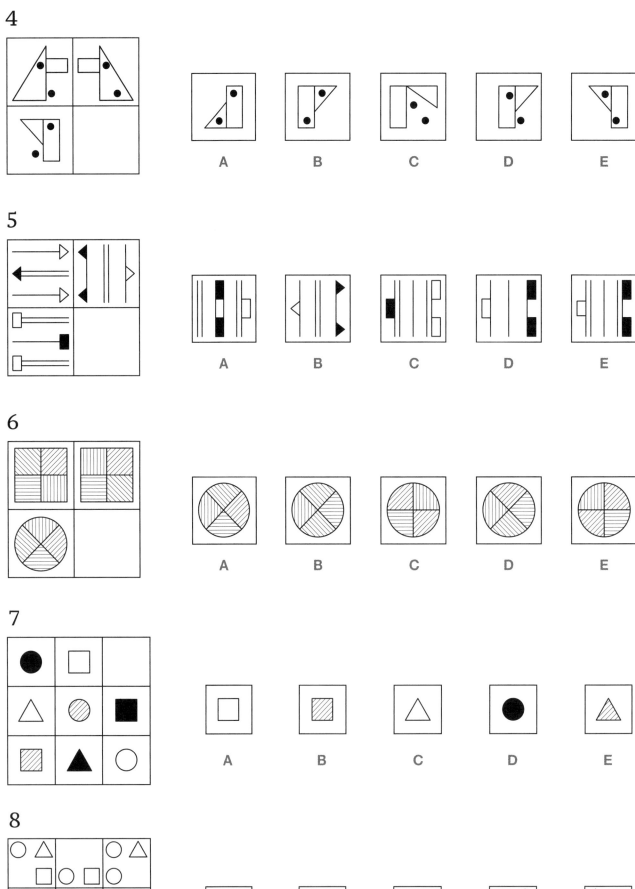

5

6

7

8

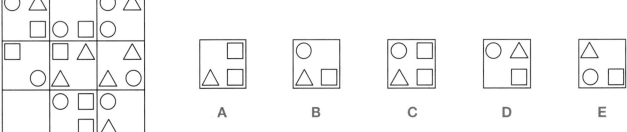

9

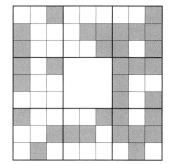

A B C D E

10

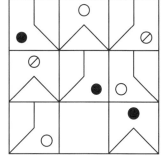

A B C D E

11

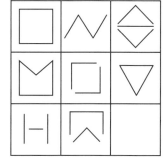

A B C D E

12

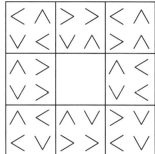

A B C D E

13

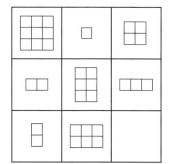

A B C D E

Merge Shapes (Hidden)

On the left is a shape. On the right, the shape can be found hidden in one of the five answer options. Circle the correct answer.

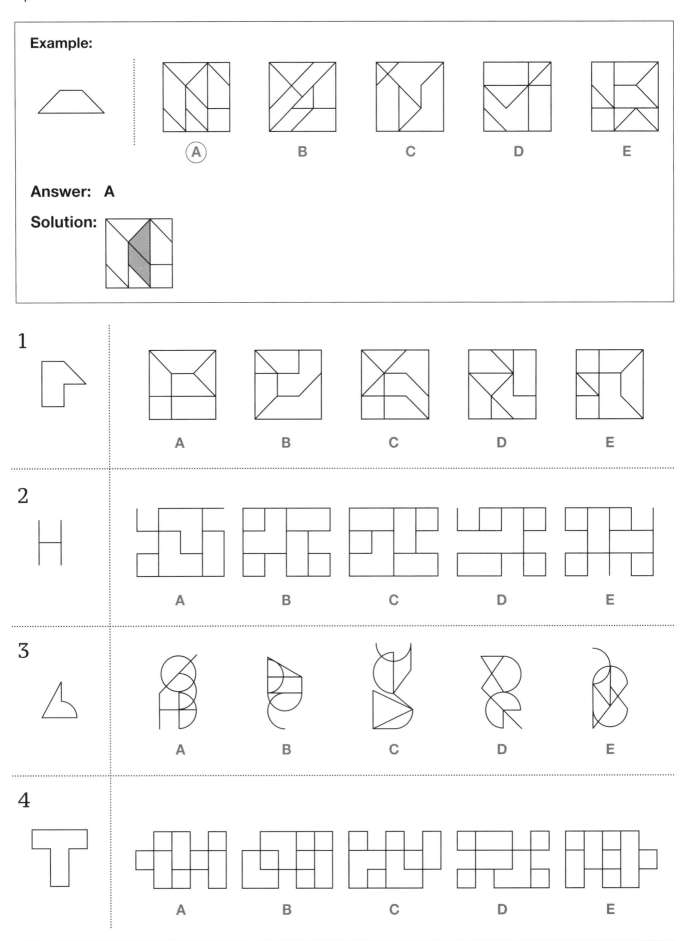

Merge Shapes (Addition)

On the left are two shapes. When they are added together they make one of the five shapes on the right. Circle the correct answer.

Example:

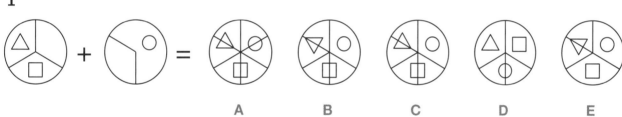

Answer: A

Solution: This diagram uses thin lines for the left-hand image and thick lines for the right-hand image or overlapping lines.

1

2

3

4

Merge Shapes (Subtraction)

On the left are two shapes. When the second one is taken away from the first, one of the five shapes on the right will remain. Circle the correct answer.

Example:

Answer: C

Solution: This diagram uses solid lines for the answer and dotted lines for what was subtracted.

1

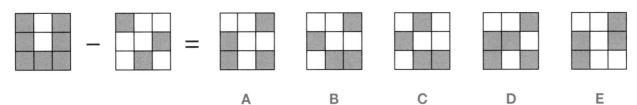

2

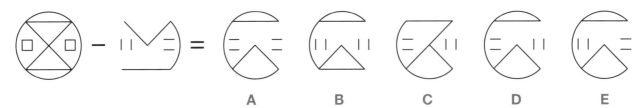

3

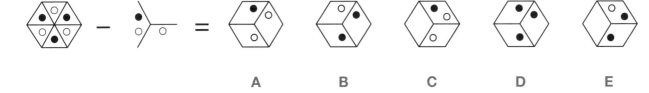

4

Cubes (Which Net?)

On the left is a cube and on the right are five nets of cubes. Only one of the nets will make the cube. Circle the correct answer.

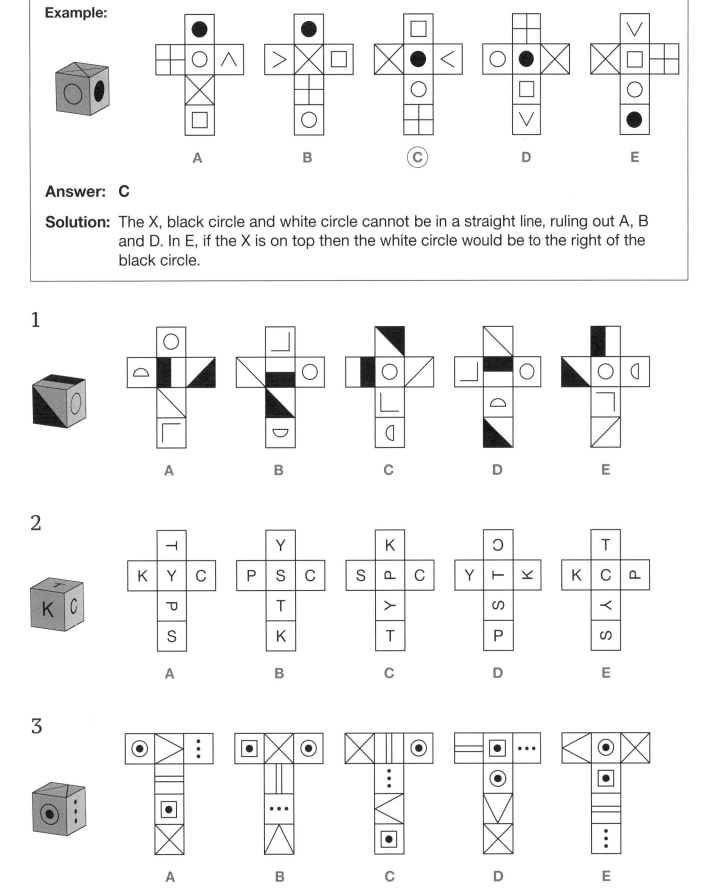

Example:

A B C D E

Answer: C

Solution: The X, black circle and white circle cannot be in a straight line, ruling out A, B and D. In E, if the X is on top then the white circle would be to the right of the black circle.

1

A B C D E

2

A B C D E

3

A B C D E

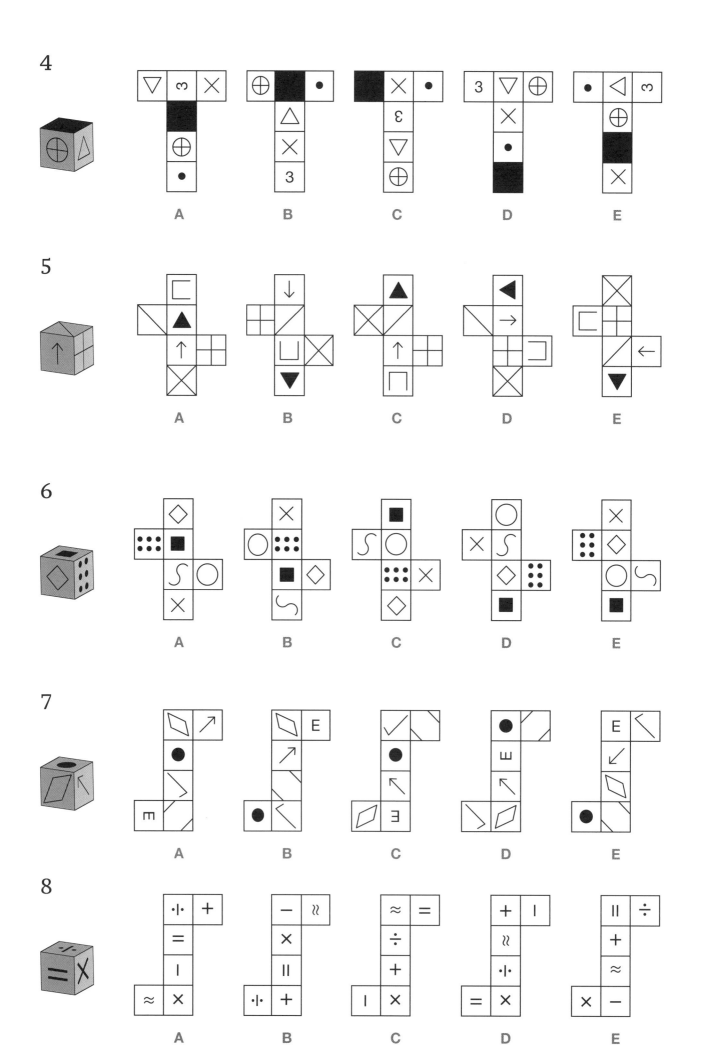

4

5

6

7

8

Cubes (Which Cube?)

On the left is a net of a cube and on the right are five cubes. One of the cubes cannot be made from the net. Circle the correct answer.

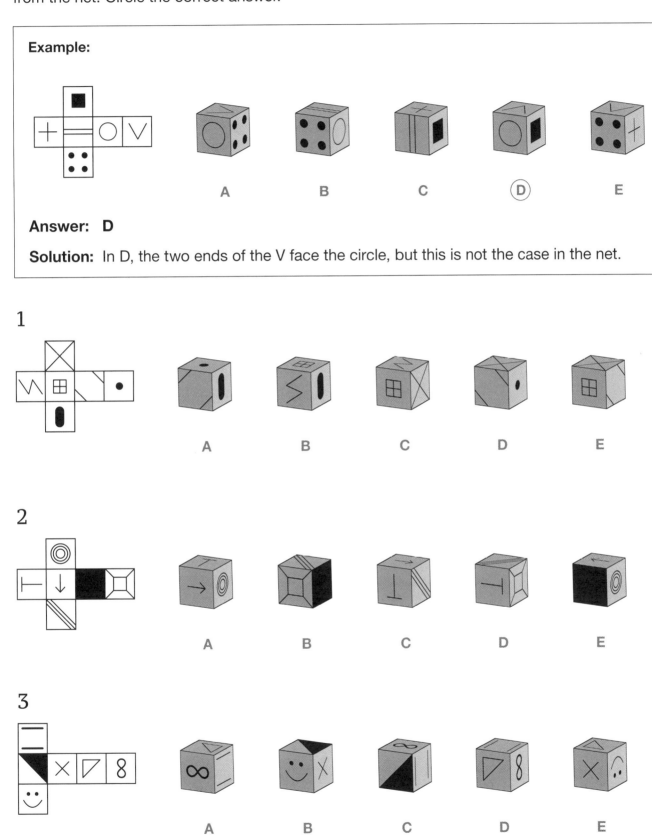

Example:

Answer: **D**

Solution: In D, the two ends of the V face the circle, but this is not the case in the net.

4

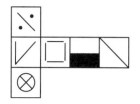

　　A　　　　　B　　　　　C　　　　　D　　　　　E

5

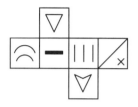

　　A　　　　　B　　　　　C　　　　　D　　　　　E

6

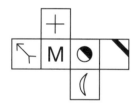

　　A　　　　　B　　　　　C　　　　　D　　　　　E

7

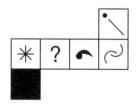

　　A　　　　　B　　　　　C　　　　　D　　　　　E

8

　　A　　　　　B　　　　　C　　　　　D　　　　　E

Folding and Punching

In the top row are images to show how a piece of paper is folded and shapes are punched into it. One of the shapes in the second row shows what the paper looks like when it is unfolded. Circle the correct answer.

Example:

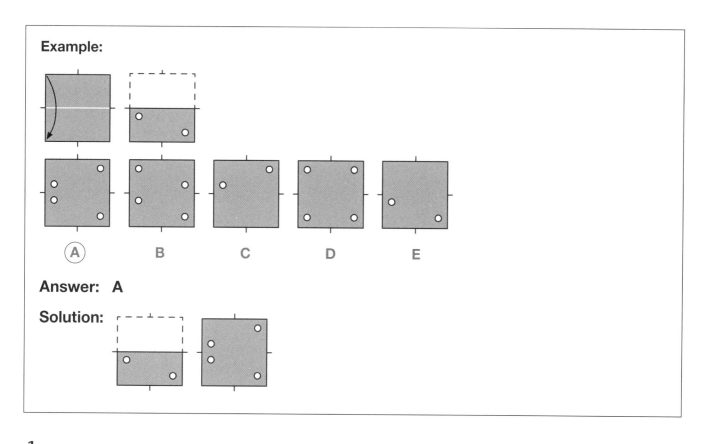

Answer: A

Solution:

1

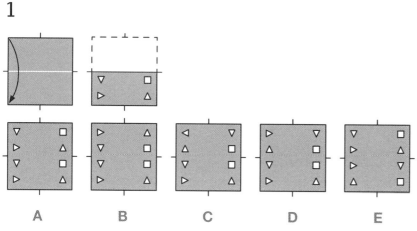

2

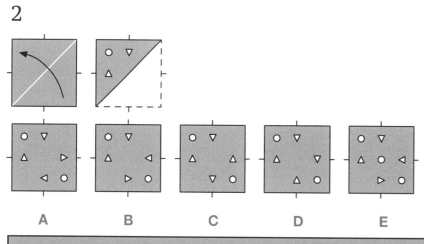

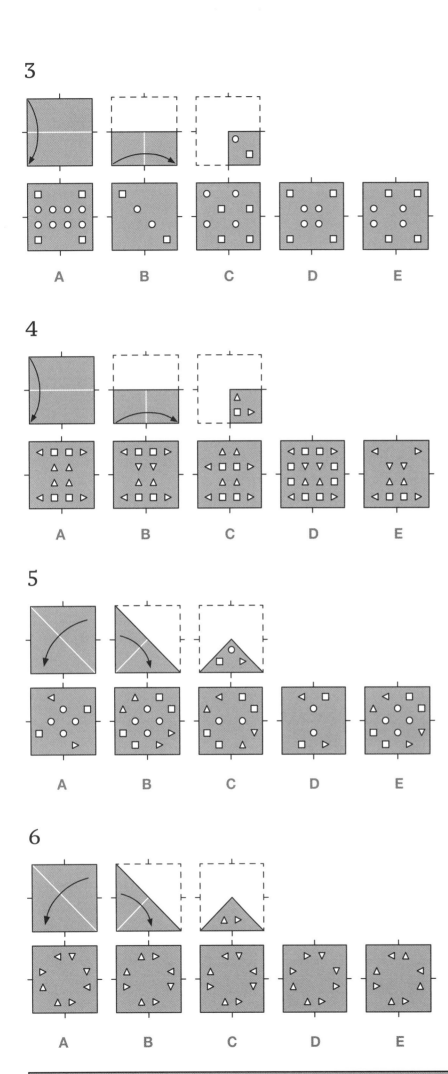

Reflections

On the left is a shape and a line of reflection. One of the five shapes on the right shows the shape when it has been reflected in the given line. Circle the correct answer.

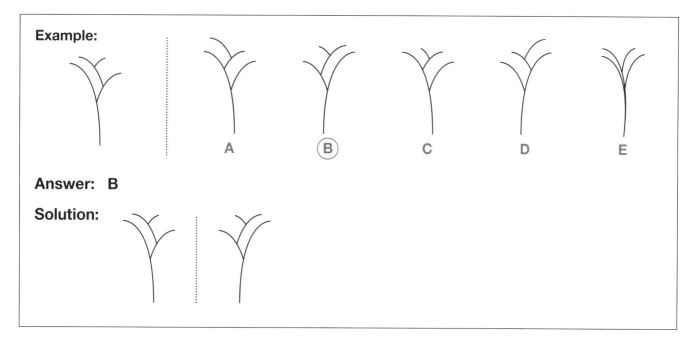

Answer: B

1

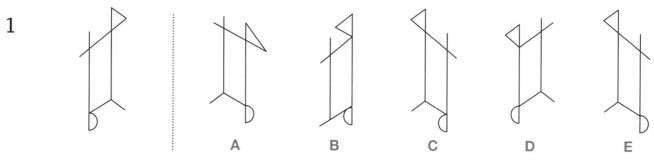

2

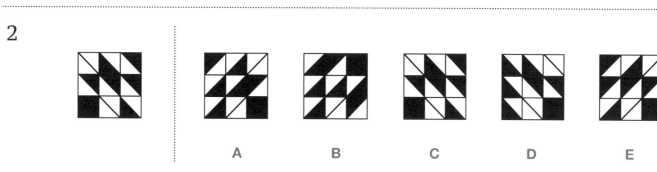

3

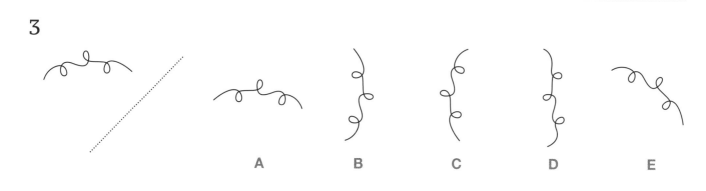

Rotations

On the left is a shape and a rotation instruction. One of the five shapes on the right shows the shape after it has been rotated by the given amount. Circle the correct answer.

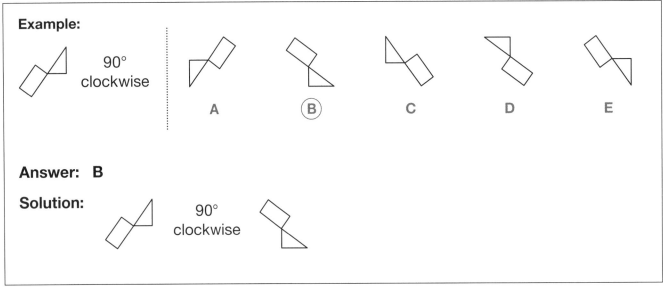

Example:

90° clockwise

A   B   C   D   E

Answer: B

Solution:

90° clockwise

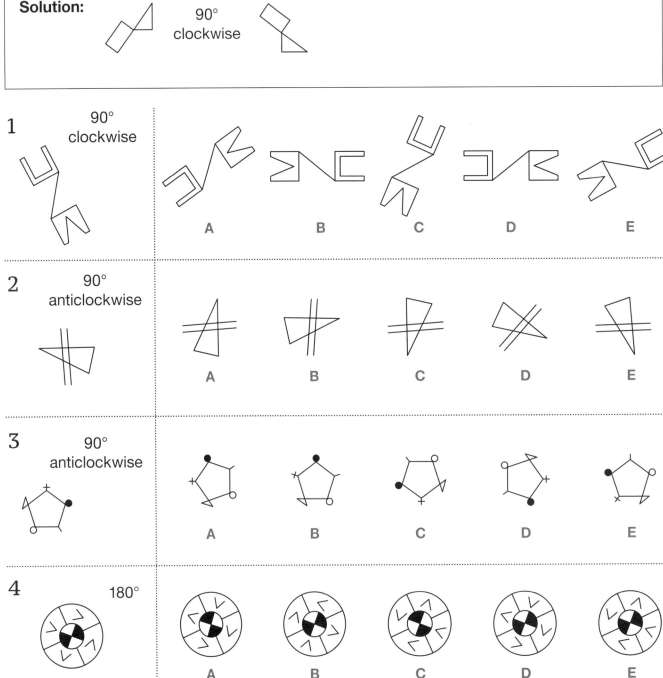

1   90° clockwise

A   B   C   D   E

2   90° anticlockwise

A   B   C   D   E

3   90° anticlockwise

A   B   C   D   E

4   180°

A   B   C   D   E

3D Shapes

On the left is a shape made up of cubes and an eye with an arrow indicating a viewing direction. One of the five plan views on the right shows the layout of cubes that would be seen from the given direction. Circle the correct answer.

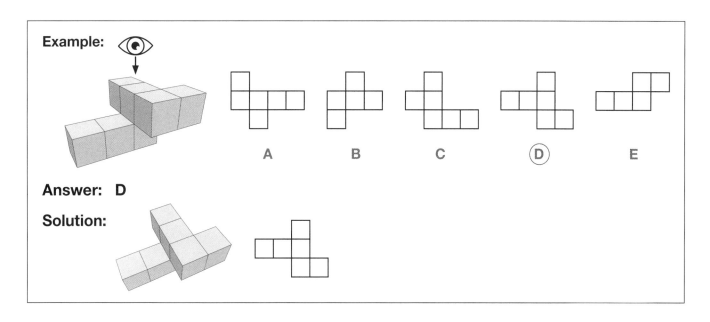

Example:

A   B   C   D   E

Answer: D

Solution:

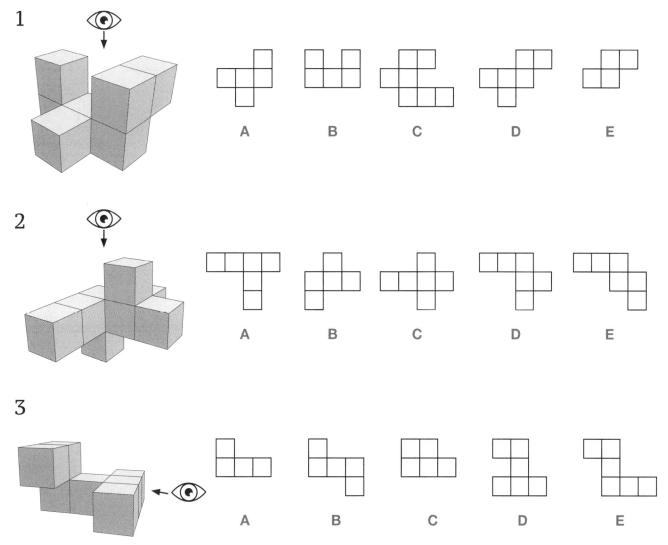

1

A   B   C   D   E

2

A   B   C   D   E

3

A   B   C   D   E

4

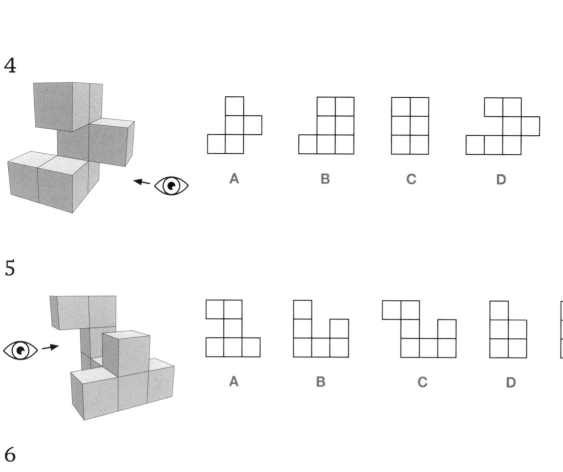

A   **B**   **C**   **D**   **E**

5

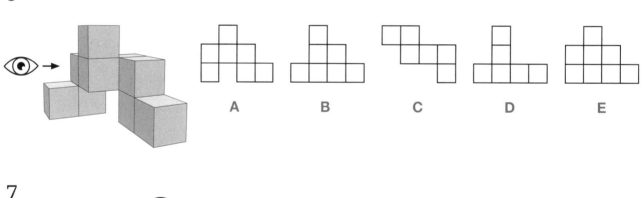

A   **B**   **C**   **D**   **E**

6

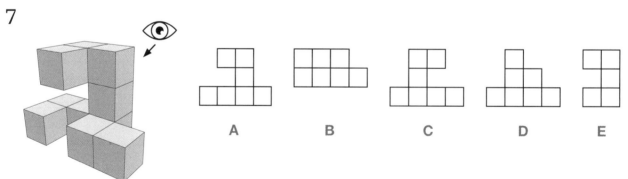

A   **B**   **C**   **D**   **E**

7

A   **B**   **C**   **D**   **E**

8

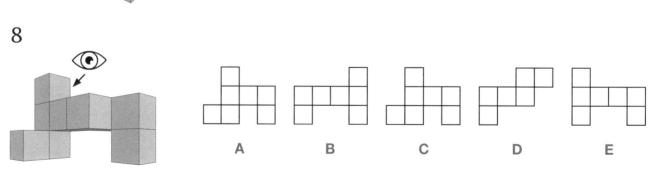

A   **B**   **C**   **D**   **E**

11+ Practice Paper 1
Non-verbal Reasoning

Information about this practice paper:

1. This paper is multiple choice. Circle your answer to each question on the test paper. If you make a mistake, rub it out and circle your new answer.

2. Pages 40–45 contain Non-verbal Reasoning questions. Read all of the questions carefully.

3. You may find some of the questions difficult. If you get stuck, go to the next question. If you are not sure, choose the answer you think is best.

4. Work as quickly and as carefully as you can.

 You have 25 minutes to complete this paper.

Merge Shapes (Addition and Subtraction)

On the left are two shapes. When they are added together, or the second one is taken away from the first, they make one of the five shapes on the right. Circle the correct answer.

Example:

○ ○
  ○ ○ **+**   ○ ○
○   ○ ○ **=**

○ ○ ○	○ ○	○ ○ ○	○ ○	○ ○ ○
○ ○	○ ○	○	○ ○	○ ○
○ ○	○ ○	○ ○ ○	○ ○ ○	○ ○
Ⓐ	B	C	D	E

Answer: A

Solution: This diagram uses thin lines for the left-hand image and thick lines for the right-hand image or overlapping lines.

○ **● ●**
  ● ○
● ●

1

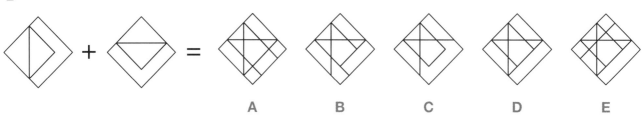

A   B   C   D   E

2

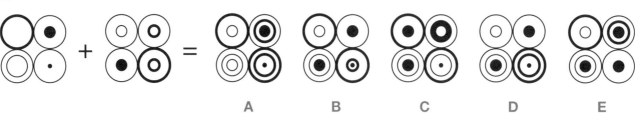

A   B   C   D   E

3

A   B   C   D   E

4

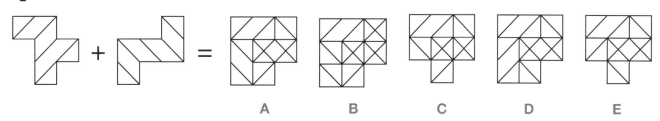

5

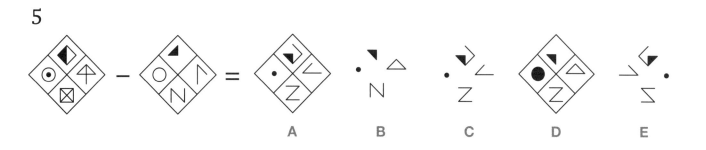

6

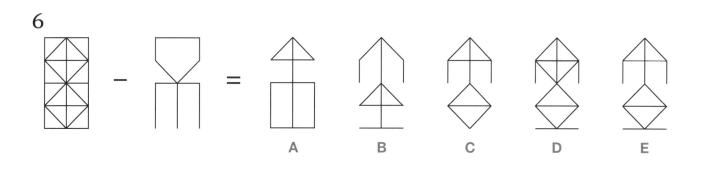

7

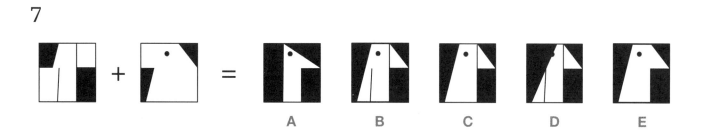

8

9

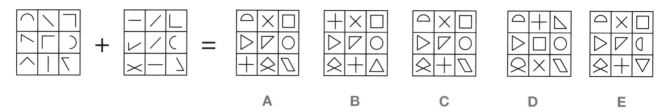

A   B   C   D   E

10

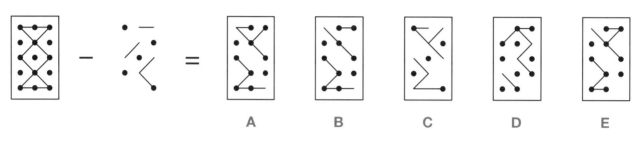

A   B   C   D   E

11

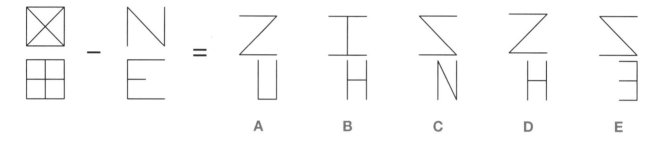

A   B   C   D   E

12

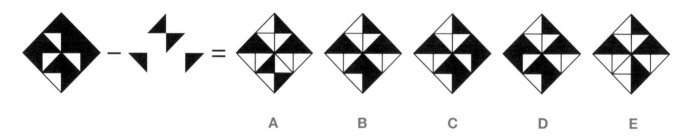

A   B   C   D   E

13

A   B   C   D   E

Series

There are five squares arranged in order with one square left empty. One of the five squares on the right replaces the empty square on the left to complete the sequence.
Circle the correct answer.

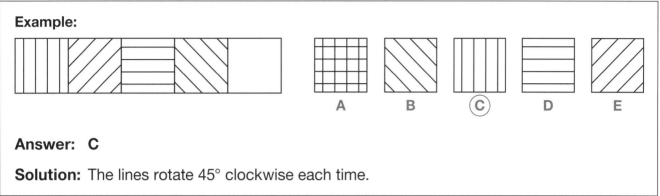

Answer: C

Solution: The lines rotate 45° clockwise each time.

14

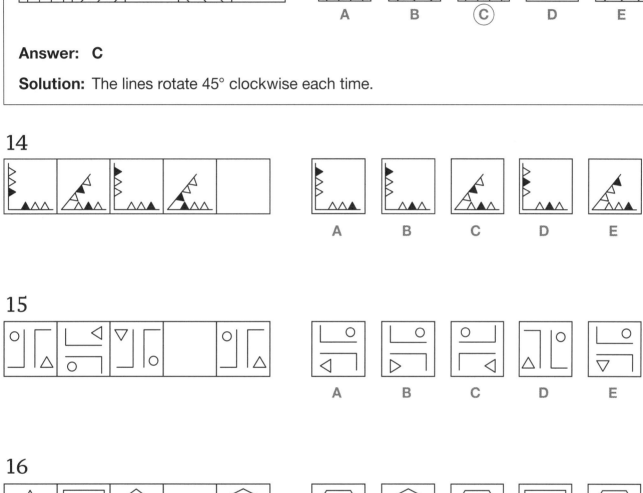

15

16

17

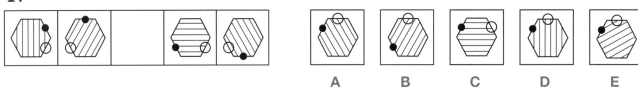

18

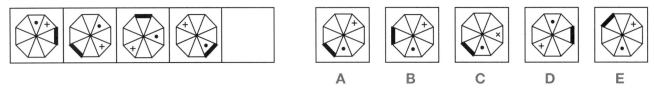

A   B   C   D   E

19

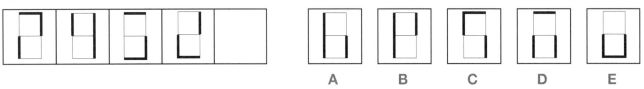

A   B   C   D   E

20

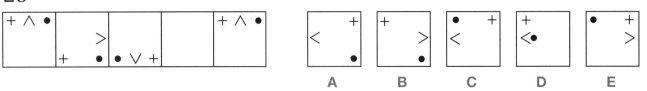

A   B   C   D   E

21

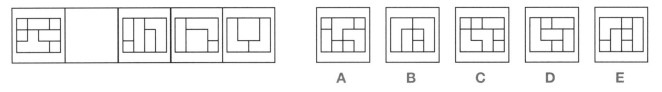

A   B   C   D   E

22

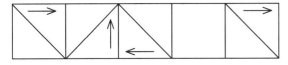

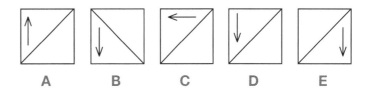

A	B	C	D	E

23

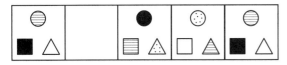

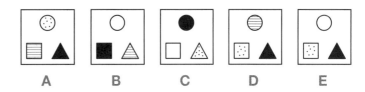

A	B	C	D	E

24

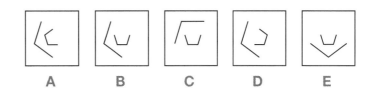

A	B	C	D	E

25

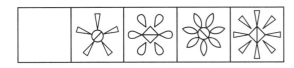

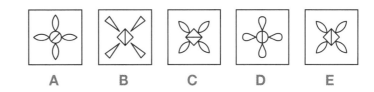

A	B	C	D	E

26

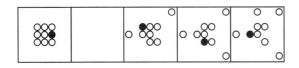

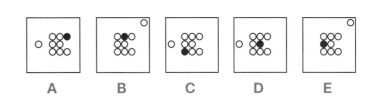

A	B	C	D	E

11+ Practice Paper 2
Non-verbal Reasoning

Information about this practice paper:

1. This paper is multiple choice. Circle your answer to each question on the test paper. If you make a mistake, rub it out and circle your new answer.

2. Pages 47–52 contain Non-verbal Reasoning questions. Read all of the questions carefully.

3. You may find some of the questions difficult. If you get stuck, go to the next question. If you are not sure, choose the answer you think is best.

4. Work as quickly and as carefully as you can.

 You have 25 minutes to complete this paper.

3D Shapes

On the left is a shape made up of cubes and an eye with an arrow indicating a viewing direction. One of the five plan views on the right shows the layout of cubes that would be seen from the given direction. Circle the correct answer.

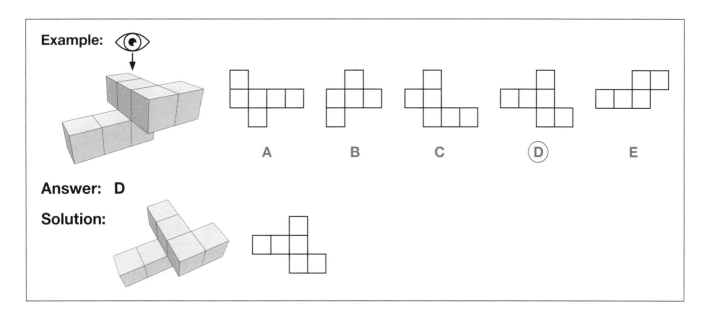

Example:

Answer: D

Solution:

1

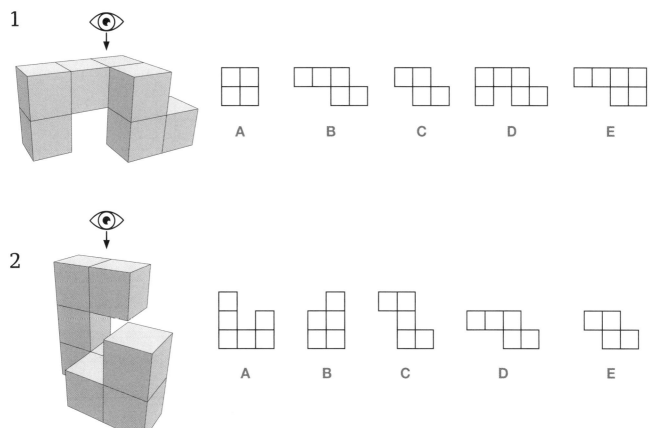

2

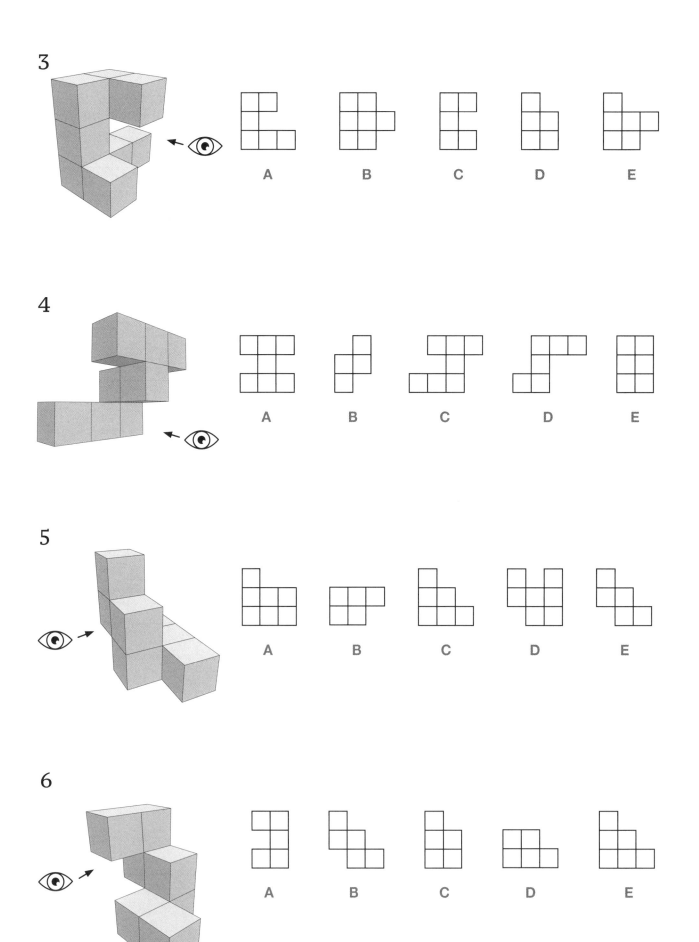

3

A B C D E

4

A B C D E

5

A B C D E

6

A B C D E

7

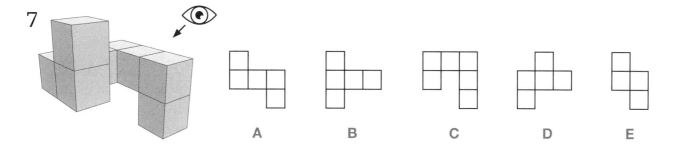

A B C D E

8

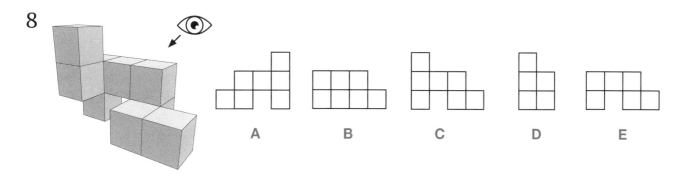

A B C D E

9

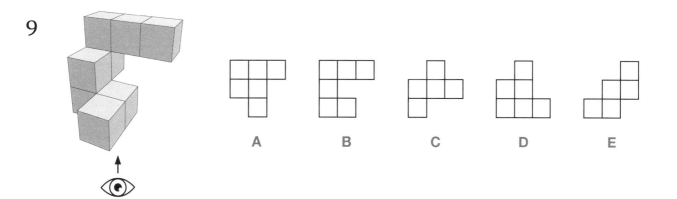

A B C D E

10

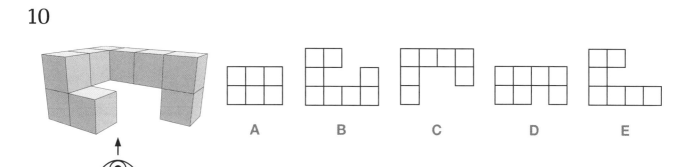

A B C D E

Analogies

On the left there are two shapes with an arrow between them. Decide what changes have been made to the shape on the left to create the shape on the right. Then look at the third shape, the arrow next to it and five more shapes. Decide which of the five shapes completes the second pair in the same way as the first pair. Circle the correct answer.

Example:

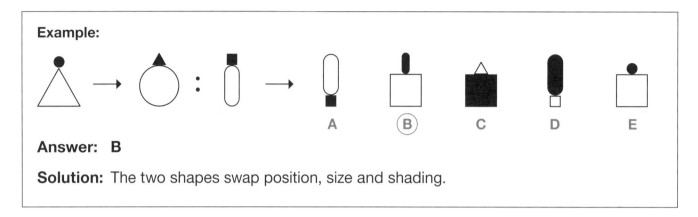

Answer: B

Solution: The two shapes swap position, size and shading.

11

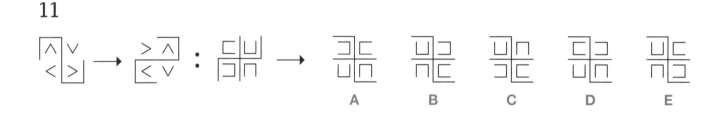

12

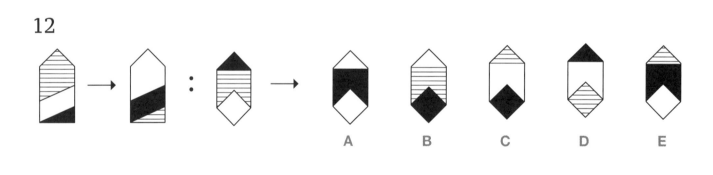

13

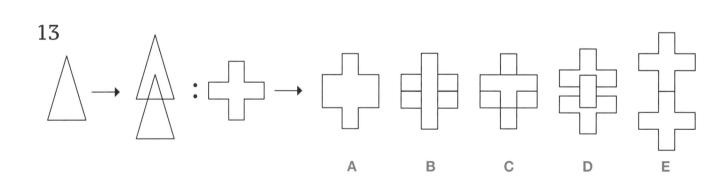

14

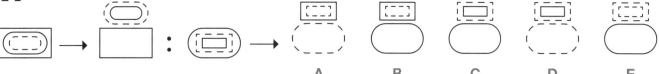

15

16

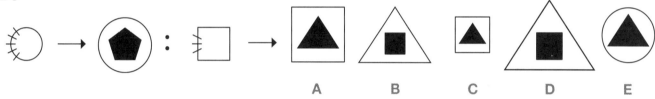

17

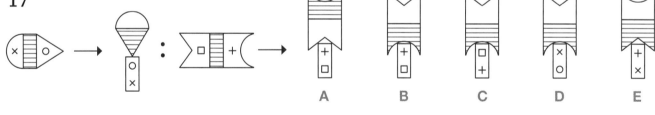

18

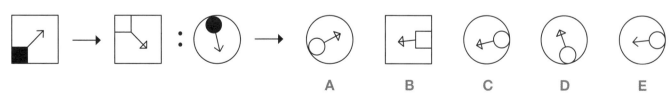

19

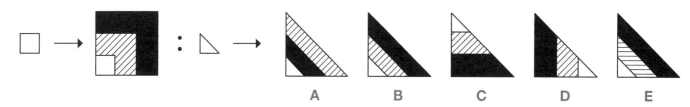

20

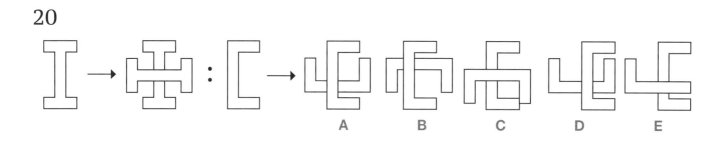

21

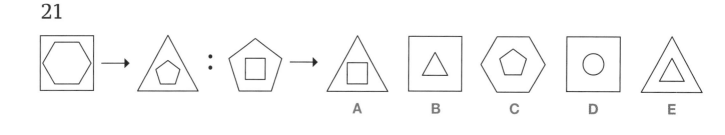

22

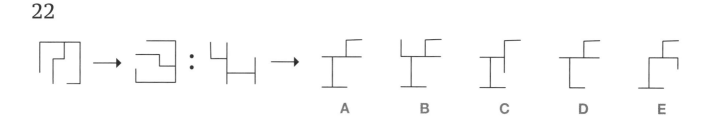

23

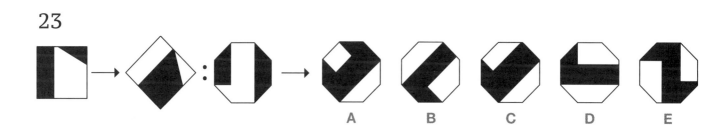

11+ Practice Paper 3
Non-verbal Reasoning

Information about this practice paper:

1. This paper is multiple choice. Circle your answer to each question on the test paper. If you make a mistake, rub it out and circle your new answer.

2. Pages 54–59 contain Non-verbal Reasoning questions. Read all of the questions carefully.

3. You may find some of the questions difficult. If you get stuck, go to the next question. If you are not sure, choose the answer you think is best.

4. Work as quickly and as carefully as you can.

 You have 25 minutes to complete this paper.

Matrices

The big square on the left contains either four or nine small squares, including one that is empty. One of the five small squares on the right will fill the empty square.
Circle the correct answer.

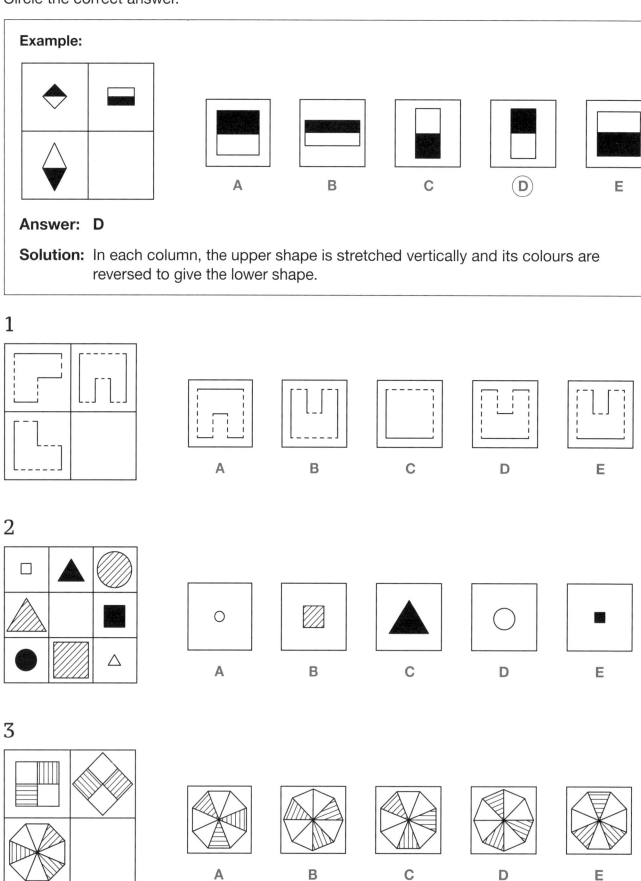

Example:

Answer: D

Solution: In each column, the upper shape is stretched vertically and its colours are reversed to give the lower shape.

1

A   B   C   D   E

2

A   B   C   D   E

3

A   B   C   D   E

4

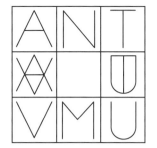

A B C D E

5

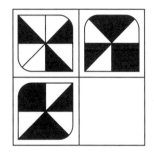

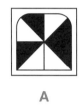    

A B C D E

6

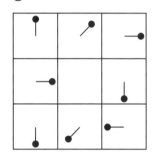

A B C D E

7

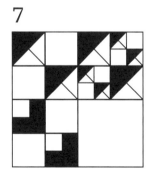

  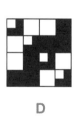 

A B C D E

8

A B C D E

9

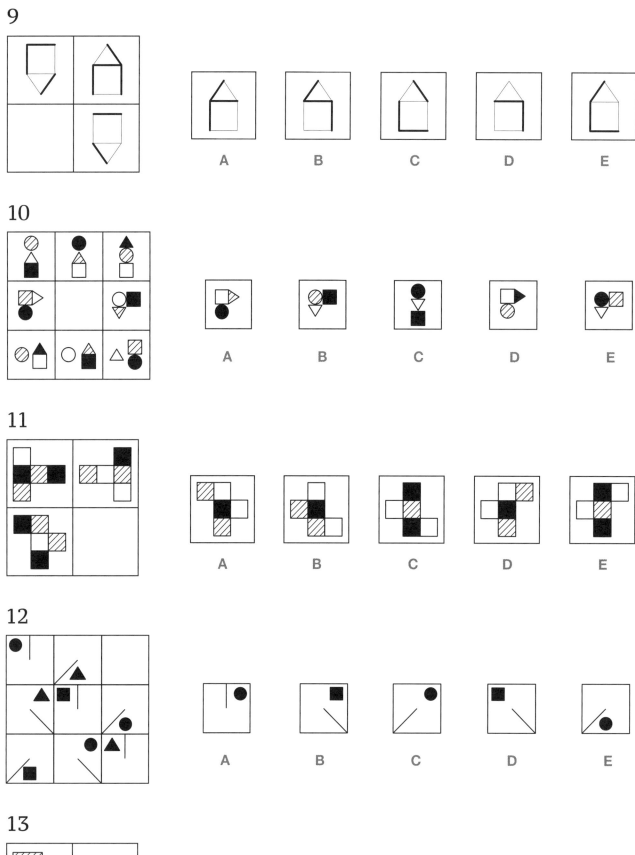

Folding and Punching

In the top row are images to show how a piece of paper is folded and shapes are punched into it. One of the shapes in the second row shows what the paper looks like when it is unfolded. Circle the correct answer.

Example:

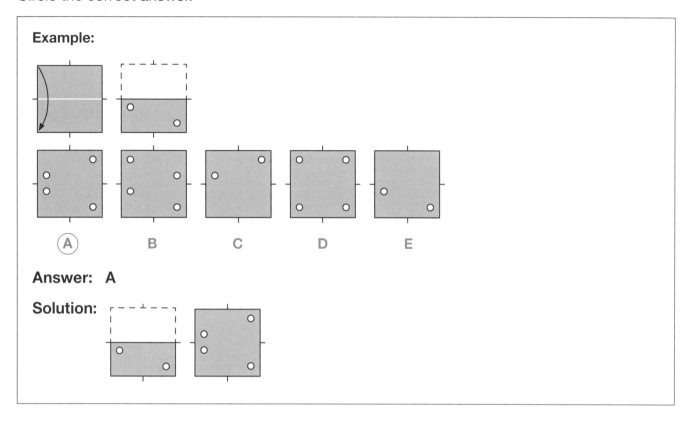

Answer: A

Solution:

14

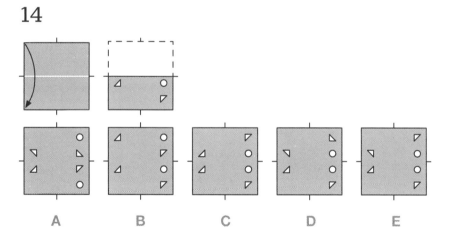

15

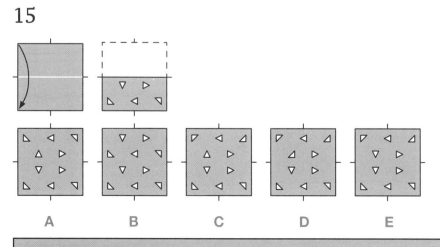

16

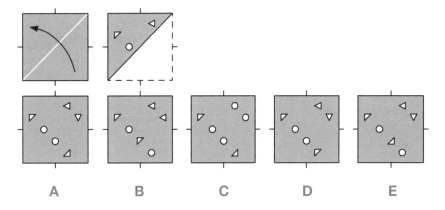

A	B	C	D	E

17

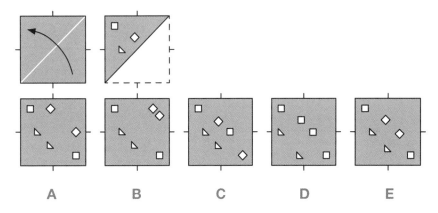

A	B	C	D	E

18

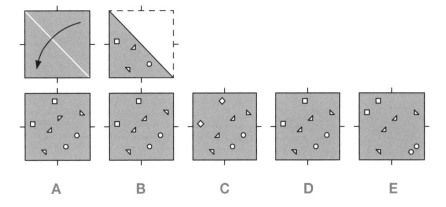

A	B	C	D	E

19

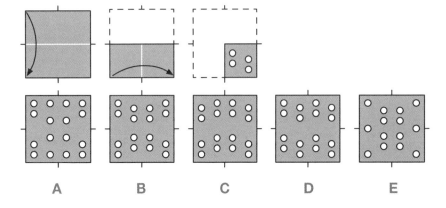

A	B	C	D	E

20

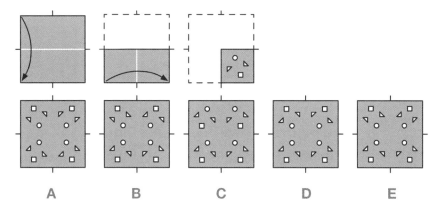

A   B   C   D   E

21

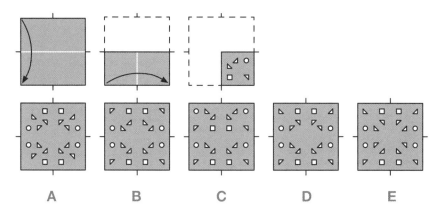

A   B   C   D   E

22

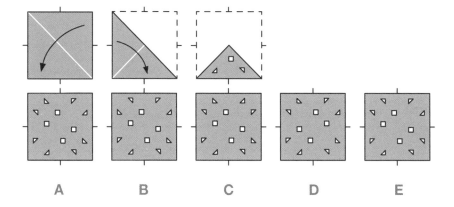

A   B   C   D   E

23

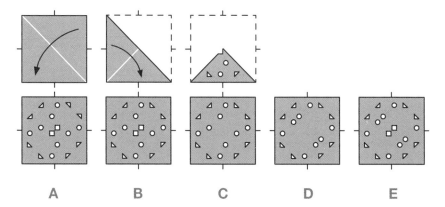

A   B   C   D   E

Answers

For extended answers including explanations, go to
www.scholastic.co.uk/pass-your-11-plus/extras/gl

Series
(pages 6–8)

1	B
2	D
3	E
4	A
5	C
6	B
7	C
8	B
9	D
10	B
11	A
12	D
13	A
14	B
15	E
16	A

Analogies
(pages 9–11)

1	C
2	E
3	A
4	B
5	D
6	C
7	A
8	C
9	E
10	B
11	D
12	A
13	E

Like Figures (Two)
(pages 12–13)

1	B
2	D
3	A
4	B
5	C
6	E
7	A
8	D

Like Figures (Three)
(pages 14–15)

1	D
2	A
3	E
4	D
5	C
6	A
7	B
8	D

Codes (In a Box)
(pages 16–17)

1	E
2	A
3	B
4	C
5	D
6	E
7	B
8	E

Codes (Two and Three Letters)
(pages 18–19)

1	C
2	E
3	B
4	E
5	C
6	B
7	A
8	D

Odd One Out
(pages 20–22)

1	C
2	D
3	A
4	E
5	D
6	B
7	C
8	C
9	B
10	D
11	A
12	E
13	B

Matrices
(pages 23–25)

1	D
2	B
3	A
4	B
5	E
6	D
7	E
8	A
9	B
10	C
11	B
12	B
13	E

Merge Shapes (Hidden)

(page 26)

1	D
2	E
3	B
4	C

Merge Shapes (Addition)

(page 27)

1	C
2	A
3	B
4	D

Merge Shapes (Subtraction)

(page 28)

1	A
2	D
3	E
4	B

Cubes (Which Net?)

(pages 29–30)

1	A
2	D
3	C
4	B
5	E
6	A
7	E
8	B

Cubes (Which Cube?)

(page 31–32)

1	C
2	A
3	D
4	B
5	E
6	C
7	A
8	B

Folding and Punching

(pages 33–34)

1	D
2	B
3	D
4	B
5	E
6	C

Reflections

(page 35)

1	C
2	E
3	B
4	A

Rotations

(page 36)

1	E
2	C
3	A
4	E

3D Shapes

(pages 37–38)

1	A
2	D
3	C
4	E
5	B
6	A
7	C
8	B

Practice Paper 1
Merge Shapes
(Addition and Subtraction)

(pages 40–42)

1	D
2	B
3	C
4	A
5	C
6	E
7	B
8	E
9	C
10	A
11	D
12	B
13	E

Practice Paper 1
Series

(pages 43–45)

14	D
15	B
16	A
17	E
18	B
19	A
20	C
21	D
22	D
23	E
24	B
25	E
26	C

Practice Paper 2
3D Shapes

(pages 47–49)

1	B
2	E
3	A
4	C
5	C
6	B
7	D
8	A
9	D
10	E

Practice Paper 2
Analogies

(pages 50–52)

11	A
12	C
13	D
14	B
15	E
16	A
17	B
18	C
19	B
20	C
21	B
22	A
23	C

Practice Paper 3
Matrices

(pages 54–56)

1	D
2	A
3	C
4	B
5	B
6	D
7	E
8	B
9	B
10	D
11	D
12	B
13	C

Practice Paper 3
Folding and Punching

(pages 57–59)

14	D
15	C
16	A
17	E
18	D
19	B
20	E
21	D
22	A
23	A

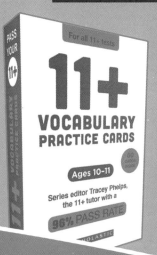